I0224641

Daddy Said

poems by

Teresa McLamb Blackmon

Finishing Line Press
Georgetown, Kentucky

Daddy Said

Copyright © 2020 by Teresa McLamb Blackmon
ISBN 978-1-64662-254-2 First Edition
All rights reserved under International and Pan-American Copyright Conventions.
No part of this book may be reproduced in any manner whatsoever without written
permission from the publisher, except in the case of brief quotations embodied in
critical articles and reviews.

ACKNOWLEDGMENTS

To those who believed that this book would happen, thank you.

In memory of my best friends and soul mates, Ralph McLamb and Cynthia
Parrish Johnson, whom I miss every day.

To my huge family, I love being another grape in the whole crazy bunch.

To my childhood friends, thanks for the sheer joy of growing up with you.

To Shelby Stephenson, for always urging me "to keep writing."

Publisher: Leah Maines

Editor: Christen Kincaid

Cover Art: Teresa McLamb Blackmon

Author Photo: Ken Tart

Cover Design: Elizabeth Maines McCleavy

Order online: www.finishinglinepress.com
also available on amazon.com

Author inquiries and mail orders:
Finishing Line Press
P. O. Box 1626
Georgetown, Kentucky 40324
U. S. A.

Table of Contents

Introduction

I have always wanted to be a poet, never a fairy princess or doctor or astronaut—a poet. Writing poetry allows me to memorialize people and places who have been treasures in my life. Several of these poems celebrate ordinary people whom I remember vividly and affectionately: piano teachers, students, even newspaper delivery boys. I wrote my first poem in the seventh grade. It was a lousy love poem. I discovered Rod McKuen in high school. He was a lousy though popular poet. I read Anne Sexton in college and was enamored by her passion for life and death. My road to poetry has been full of route-changes and detours.

Writing poetry has given me a way to examine relationships, especially those involving my father. Poems about my father are not chronological for a reason. My feelings about him have been conflicted. Some days he is my hero; some days he is just human.

What a joy it has been to write about my childhood. Growing up in a small town with a crowd of neighborhood friends and cousins guarantees incredible memories. We cruised Main, jumped in farm ponds when dared, and played Spin the Bottle too often. I praise Main Streets, mules, Blue Horse notebook binders, Green Stamps and fat, red pencils in the first grade.

As I near senior citizen status, I have begun to consider my life and my imminent death. I have lived a great life and death is not something I dread. It is something for which I want to be prepared. Several poems came about because of the death of some of my best friends at far too early an age. Whether dead or alive, whether near or far away, whether hero or human, the people appearing in these poems must not be forgotten. I cannot let them go.

These are honest poems about real people and real experiences. They are about a life and a time I yearn to share with you and all who come after.

"Maybe being a Southern writer is only a matter of loving a damaged and damaging place, of loving its flawed and beautiful people, so much that you have to stay here, observing and recording and believing, against all odds, that one day it will finally live up to the promise of its own good heart."

Margaret Renkle,"What is a Southern Writer, Anyway?"

"Someone needs to tell those tales. When the battles are fought and won and lost, when the pirates find their treasures and the dragons eat their foes for breakfast with a nice cup of Lapsang souchong, someone needs to tell their bits of overlapping narrative. There's magic in that. It's in the listener, and for each and every ear it will be different, and it will affect them in ways they can never predict. From the mundane to the profound. You may tell a tale that takes up residence in someone's soul, becomes their blood and self and purpose. That tale will move them and drive them and who knows what they might do because of it, because of your words. That is your role, your gift.
Erin Morgenstern, "The Night Circus"

Barning Tobacco

Tobacco sleds brush sand
like a child with a stick on the beach,
idly going about his business.
At sun-up, the barn crew dreads the sticky gum

of night's dew on leaves.
Peggy Alford strings the 'bakker, whips it in place,
races with Brenda Parker to yell "stick off" and waits
for the boys to come and send it up to barn tiers.

A ritual of mules bringing loads of leaf to
women singing "Itsy Bitsy Teeny Weeny Yellow Polka Dot Bikini,"
and "Judy's Turn to Cry."
Gather, reach, loop, stick, poke it up, and then again

until the sun reaches 10:00 and Daddy sends Rebecca
to the store—
no feast no better than R. C. Colas and square nabs.
The children at the barn play in dirt,

making imaginary horses from tobacco sticks to ride
as far as summer heat will take them.
Daddy lets them come, if they stay out of the way.
Their mamas work tobacco leaves into a frenzy

of green. Their daddies off in the field, count
rows and rounds 'til break or lunch or quit'n time.
Jean Norris eats junk so long she gets "knick-knack colic,"
Daddy calls it.

When the workday ends, the croppers come out of
fields like survivors from a meaningless war,
the stringers and the handers and the young'uns
clear the barn, no singing now, just a straight shot

to the back of the pickup.
Those that can, sit with feet dangling
off the tailgate, reaching for pavement or
dirt, as if they could stop

the Ford, the "wearies" or the next day's crop.
When Friday comes, the little ones watch
as the pay covers their parents' gummed-stamped hands,
just enough for school clothes or groceries,

a light bill or charge account at Reuben Barbour's Grocery.
They tag along to town,
hoping to see ends meet.

Daddy Said

"Keep knocking along. Gotta buy the baby some shoes."

"Son, have you got a girlfriend? Does she have a pretty mother?"

"I've 'bout give out but I've not give up."

"Son, stand your ground."

When he goes to bed at night, I hear him praying,
mumbling like he does when he figures up Friday payroll,
(fingers at work and a pencil with a knife-whittled lead.)

He's talking to God, the original "Old Buddy,"
settling up.

Seasons End

This might be the year of leaving,
this time when nothing has the leisure of waiting.
Tree branches bare, a little fox scurries
for fish perished on the dam.
The moon, perched on sky smooth as a tabletop,
sits like an empty cup to be filled.
Dusk brings the smell of earth,
as farmers return to fallow fields,
pull up the fruits of vine,
swiftly yanking roots and stems
as if the planting had been a mistake.
I live in this picture, a shadow near the bottom,
hovering like the catfish in winter mud.

Originally published in *Poet Lore*, Vol. 106, Number 3/4

Uncles

We can't imagine them
anything but uncles,
men who rode us on their knees
and called us "Baby" beyond our forties
We've heard the tales: of plowing
with mules and sneaking
cigarettes in the corn crib,
of Mama and Papa and Sunday dinners,

of hog killings, of sneaking
pies from the pie safe,
or sop chocolate for
breakfast and apple jacks for dessert.

We know they wore starched
white shirts to Dogeye,
the old one-room schoolhouse,
and we know that Papa traded

mules in the old stables downtown.
We've seen the newspaper photos
of four sons in a world war
at the same time. We know they served

proudly and returned to talk about
Fort Bragg and the medics and the time
one brother ran into the other in a field hospital.

We grow older and see ourselves
turning into them like leaves change
in their time to what they have
to be in Autumn.

Each of us has one of their quirks:
shaking popcorn and peanuts
in our hands, then aiming
for the mouth, nephews' hands in pocket,

whistling tunes made up through
tobacco middles and cotton rows.
We just can't imagine that they were little
tots comforted in a mother's arms, that they

had mumps and measles and broken hearts,
that they ever lay in bed afraid
of the dark or feared
the boogey man who might have hid

in the old outhouse—these brothers who leave us now,
one by one like mischievous boys
who run to play and refuse
to come when called.

Orignially published in *The McKinley Review*, Issue 6, Summer 2019

A Child's Delivery

I could never forget the climb,
tedious as Jack and the Beanstalk's journey,
into the pickup truck where Daddy waited,
brimmed hat bent down, blue eyes
watching for me.

We slipped through town, partners
with the yellow thief, to rob the
dew and set the day afoot.

"One quart for the Lamberts," he'd say,
"and two for Old Man Webb."

Families slept, unaware that a child
had come to bring the milk,
and a father watched, knowing that
the empty bottles left
would come back to him.
My tiny hands would reach again,
like Jack, for the way home.

Shared Lessons

(For Shannon)

So fragile she was there in her desk,
writhing in a life as tangled as Medusa's locks—
the little girl who was a shadow of pain,
a whisper longing for a careful voice,
assigned to me that year.

The journals she kept held her together,
gave the fears a place to live, to breathe
until they could escape. Following the breadcrumbs
of sages and quests of poets and wanderers,
she took off, certain of her path—

Now she finds me pushing questions around,
like old homeless women who move their lives
from stoop to stoop to find a temporary home.
I have become her student, certain
that there are answers.

Last Request

When Daddy dies, I want a black topped table,
one some sophomore used for biology experiments,
the smell of formaldehyde to stifle me.
I want safety glasses so I can see
all that's there before me.
I will take the T-pins and hold his old body down.
I have waited all my life to see what lies beneath
his skin, what holds these bones together, what words
unsaid might spill freely from his speechless tongue.
I need no partner for this. I will stand over him; I will
have him where I want him. He will listen now.
I do not want to see the blue eyes. I want empty
sockets that I can dig into. I want dumb lips and ears,
no foul-fake terms of endearment.
I want to fit my fat fleshy fingers into
the sticks of his hands. I want his crunchy knuckles
to beat upon mine. I need that music, the percussion
of nothingness.
I want to pick up his skull and hold it in my hands.
I want to look at it in wonder, rattle it—
The parts that worked his heart, his judgment,
His wayward feet.
His grey matter will not be fleshy like the summer's watermelon;
it will be rotten, like the Fall.
I want to open his empty mouth and see what fed him,
what satisfied his soul, what stuck to the roof of his mouth.
I want to cut out the kneecaps, smooth them out like worn pebbles
and carry them in my pockets. I want to touch them
when I reach for coins or grocery lists.
I want to paint his rib cage blue for town sparrows
that can fly only as far as the frame lets them.
One by one I'll crack the bones
and free them.
They will flutter past his lungs and heart
while I watch.

Originally published in *Toasted Cheese Literary Journal*, March 2019.

"Knock on Wood"

Growing up in a small town-cruisin' Main
with Otis Redding singing on the radio,
dreading teachers with names like Pansy and Wilhelmenia,

walking the whole of Main Street, never
meeting a stranger, watching tobacco worms
slither through plowed middles

and silly boys biting them in half for girly screams,
going to Miss Johnny Green's store to buy candy cigarettes
knowing she'd never tell when we bought the real thing,

making sand castles at Carolina Beach, melting
dozens of Britt's famous doughnuts
through sun-scorched lips,

crying when the week was over at Camp Don Lee,
playing spin the bottle, taking kisses
in Miss Louise Godwin's living room closet,

eating cherry pies we honestly believed "Miss" Lily
 made from scratch, rushing home after Sunday church
for what was fried and fattening,

cruising Charlie's Carousel in a Caprice station wagon,
learning about sex at a Friday night pajama party
and not believing a word of it.

All in an Ordinary Day

A mare is down, the foal won't come.
Daddy knew it but said she'd be okay,
his usual, "Oh, she'll be alright," what he said to me
when I'd call home from Raleigh telling him I didn't want
to live anymore: "Be a big girl. You'll be alright."

He said that to a 37-year old daughter.
The vet came and we watched him
tie chains to the unborn feet.
He felt no heartbeat in the womb
and pulled to save the older life.

We could do nothing but watch, knowing that the mare
was only bearing death, but there was a whimper:
the colt grabbed breath. Even the vet had tears.
Up all night, we watched the downed mother
still lying in the mud, weak from the effort, too

weak to even look over at her baby.
Next day, the mare died, and we fed the foal
with baby bottles—two days he sipped
at life, but couldn't swallow it. Another death.
I paid the vet bill, buried the mother and son

and waited for Daddy to explain all this away.

Orginally published in *Floyd County Moonshine,* Vol. 11, Issue 1, Spring 2019.

Impatient Bait

It was not the jump that scared me,
kept me stone-still, frozen in sun.
I knew the air was quick
like slick, supple hands.
I could bear the bounce, could look
down and know I would find water.

It was the landing, not sure
that the plunge would take me
to the bottom and up again with breath
to spare. I was falling into something
bigger than myself,
something that would surround me
yet leave too much room.

Fear schooled me, swam me
like circling bubbles in the bathtub drain, me
so afraid of leaving the board, I'd bob
up and down like impatient bait,
watching myself in the blue mirror,
seeing a stranger I knew so well.

7th Grade

We all have first loves, puppy
love that may be silly but real
to the puppy. I was no different,
sure, in the 7th grade, that my life
would depend on a kiss
from the lips of David Dunn,
and it did.

Like an unexpected snowfall:
there is bare, cold ground,
clouds pout, waiting,
and suddenly, at dawn,
everything is different, silent, pure
covered by tiny white fingers,
turned into something
it had never been before.

Aunt Pauline at 83

She fishes for a living,
finds her wallowed spot on the pond dam,
squirms her legs to the place
they fit down the bank.
She sits right on the edge, a little sprite,
as if the pond is there because of her.
With her a cane pole, catalpa worms, and
resolve as big as any yellow cat she'll catch.

We look out our comfortable window and wonder
how she stays put, hooking bass and bream
one after another,
breaking her line, repairing it,
sipping ice water from a quart jar in a cooler shared with chilled bait.
She just waits for the nibble, the bite-
no worry that one might get away.
There is a reckoning. Some are baited, some
Turn away. Only a few will be fit to keep.
She fishes for a living, throws the line as far
as she can and holds onto it,
satisfied with the pull that keeps her alive.

Orginally published in *Noctua Review*, Vol. XII, 2019

Losing Ralph

You can't possibly be gone from the city.
You've been taken by a fanatic
who thinks you're John Boy,
or held by some nefarious terrorist.
You've lost your way in the subway—
That's it!
You are riding the Broadway Local
from Columbus Circle to 14th Street,
not sure whether it's Sandalino's omelets
or Li Lac's chocolates you want.
As night cruises Christopher,
you know it is Five Oaks and Marie you seek.
Just once more you need to hear her
"Sam You Made the Pants too Long" or
some redneck tourist request "New York, New York."
You yearn to know that her tight braids,
and frantic fingers are still making music,
breath-taking songstress of sunrise.
No matter what they say,
I know you are there somewhere.
I will find you.
At Rockefeller Center I will hold
a stranger's hand and tiptoe on ice.
They will guide me along until I've checked
every frozen face and foot and blade.

Edward Perry

Hidden with local briefs:
"Long-time hawker of the *News & Observer* dies at 81."

Children snickered at the sight of him,
bent and broken, dragging his life
and the daily news through the streets,
then to a faded canvas bag draping his uncertain shoulders.
He was a statue of habit, reliable and stoic
as the war heroes permanent in the park.
Routing through side streets and store entrances,
he was an obstacle in the night—
something one knows is there
and without thinking, steps around.

Now the story is his, a single paragraph among
scattered print on Tuesday's floor:
A sister says he walked himself to death,
ten miles to his downtown beat.
A department store clerk says
he counted his change every day, persistent
and precise, asking her to verify with
the calculators she sold at her counter.
His preacher says he sorted the coins
in paper rolls and gave his tithe to God.
He liked order and routine.
He knew headlines from years before,
his own circulation statistics: the facts.
He stood there, seldom changing
as the news did, watching us
heavily burdened by our own
rolled and tossed lives,
carelessly landing helter skelter.
We wondered what happened to
him, never a name 'til now,
just the little paper man with
his time-clock routine
Wound as tight as a deadline.

Hair-Do

Sitting still on Saturdays, wedged between
Mama's legs, on the edge of a rattan ottoman,
my head tilted and turned, like someone looking for a noise,
while my mother pin curled my hair.
She twirled with her thumb and forefinger,
making a circle as fat and tight as a grub worm,
stabbed it with first one bobby pin and then another,
the shape of a cross.
I was only five or six and sitting there
a solid hour for a few curls
that mother would ruffle for Sunday School.
She was proud of the ringlets and waves
and her little girl who tried
to believe that she was "precious in His sight."

Teenage Redemption

We collected Barbie doll clothes and Sunday School pins.
We saved pennies for candy and dollars
for those crazy photos in beach arcade booths.
We sold lemonade and loom-looped potholders
in well-groomed front yards
and gave up our earnings to play
pop machines and pinball.
We kept S & H Green Stamps in Pappagallo shoe boxes,
and clipped Blue Horse coupons from blue cloth binders.

We knew about redemption even then,
saving our youth like cookies in holiday tins.
We meet now in beaches of our past, laugh at
cotton candy dreams and tide-racing desires.
We show our hands on card tables our mothers used
for bridge club.
We play "What Could Have Been"
like we played Old Maids and Crazy Eights.
We play by the rules now; wear bifocals to read them.

From Where I've Been

When dark has beat her home,
four geese hover over goslings,
warm them like blankets

they might become,
three donkeys, in prayer-like ritual,
bend to the ground for grain,

too busy to bray
or lift long ears.
Two pups awaken

and blend their bark
with familiar gravel
under wheels coming or going.

One man inside has no idea
the distance she has been, beneath
grazing stars with water watching.

Originally published in *From the Edge Poetry Magazine*, Spring 2019

Thanatopsis in Mind

So wait, in this persistent vegetative state,
lying there, mouth clinched pouty like a child,
knuckles stretched in a purgatorial grip.
Wait, while doctors and nurses enter.

Wait with family-gathered photographs
left standing guard, Kodachromatic sentinels
pursuing your blue-eyed glance,
sent to fetch you back
from the no-place you've been.

Wait, while visitors disturb your
wrap of stillness, mumbling prayers
like conversation heard through thin walls
as if there is someone listening
on the other side of silent.

Wait until that caravan of saints parades by,
sustained and soothed by an unfaltering trust,
falls in place. Match them step for step.
March until you hear their beat and
recognize the melody we do not hear.

Your wait is over.
Go now.
Take your seat with the stars.

Quick Work

Just as they've done every summer,
the couple watches the arrival
of hummingbirds, winged-motor
of spring, sugar-water thirsty
near big bay windows,
quick, sassy fights over a front-porch perch.

In August heat, they see feathers
court over blooms
of geraniums and crepe myrtles,
and imagine the music of such speed,
the diligence of quick work,
the complacency of sipping
so little and moving on.

Big Folks Table

The unbelievably high sliding board
is now just a kiddy toy in a tiny park.
The long ride to Grandma's is a quick
trip on the backroads. The inviting
big folks' table at Christmas
seems tight and uncomfortable.

The heartbreak of puppy love
now feels silly, and failing a spelling test,
once life-threatening, just a nuisance.
The first scary speeding ticket
has become a funny story to share.

All the frightening hurdles of life
become minor irritations, like summer flies,
when held up against the terror
of days with nothing to fret
about but the gigantic nothingness to come.

Henrietta

With her hands by her side,
lips pursed in pure-t-pleasure,
she feeds ten cats, pampers
an insurance man who drinks
and gambles, and raises children
to believe they can beat the odds
as she does the back-porch rug
where the Weimaraner lies
keeping the screen door company—the door
she slams when no one is home to hear.

With her hands on her hips,
feet shuffling worn pink scuffs
through the kitchen, she cooks
peas, beans and yams,
bringing workers from fields,
arranging plates on a table,
bowls as big as buckets.
Knives and spoons take their places
like well-mannered children,
in a room with little space.

With her hands holding her chin,
she preens the feathers of her worth,
head tilted to a mirror
that Camel smoke encircles
as a dance partner might.
Henrietta's Saturday night—
to dinner, to dance, to
drape night air like a stole
around her shoulders,
hands free, hips swinging.

With her hands on her partner's shoulder
she moves gently as if it's the first time
dancing. But it is not her first
dance nor is it a man she knows.

For once she steps out
and swirls in circles, unfamiliar
yet freeing. When the music stops,
she knows she will sway
like this again.

With her hands in her pockets,
she departs this place. Once outside,
she lights a cigarette, mesmerized
by the smoke around her face.
She blows away this fog,
seeing clearly now that she
no longer needs an image
to see herself. This night
has brought her to her feet.
She has amazing moves.

Tender Shoots

It is a terrible thing wishing
to die, just when the spring
blooms are birthing
and tender shoots break dirt.

Yes, a desperate thing to give up
waiting, believing in gods
and fairies. Finally, to say
"Aw, shucks," it isn't worth

the wait, toss out the leftovers,
ignore spare change.
Just when God is in
His Heavens, what a disgrace

to stay put and wait
for all the nothingness
that, like spring green grass,
has been growing underneath all the while.

The Blue Top: 1960

Outside the Blue Top service station
on the corner of Main and 301, middle-aged
men balance on empty Cola crates,
sit hunched over, elbows to knees,

work-stained hands full of chins. Hats and caps
tilted ever-which-a-way, fit heads all full
of a day's work or next week's intentions.
Stained fingers flick burned-out butts, glowing

fireflies in the night air as Camels
and Lucky Strikes send smoke
in circles of angry clouds. Old timers
spit with the accuracy of rain.

Those that can, whistle,
and every one of them snorts and coughs
and reaches for soiled handkerchiefs
in pockets filled with case knives, penny mints

and loose change.
Their conversation rarely varies, only
when the weather does. Never enough or too much,
rain, wind, heat.
They brag about garden plots and tobacco crops,

their new mule, their old Chevy. Their voices buzz
and nag like mosquitoes. Fibs and exaggerations
punctuate their chatter, a steady beat.
It's as if they're keeping score—who works

the hardest, catches the biggest,
remembers the most, or finishes first.
Their stories play like songs we love to hate.
About closing time, they ante up

Releasing coins that ring as they fall
into the fat red Coke machine
next to windshield wipers, motor oil and maps.
Pulling Cokes,

checking thick bottle bottoms for their origin,
making small bets they can afford.
They grab their drink from the red machine,
walk away as nonchalant as cats at rest.

They check their luck as if it doesn't matter.
First one shouts "Raleigh," a sure loser,
and then "Pittsburgh, Chicago," a Fayetteville or two.
The farther away the better—

five or six case quarters and a palm-spread
of nickels and dimes. They argue over mileage
for a spell, put their crates away
and head home, just down the street.

Originally published in *Toasted Cheese Literary Journal*, March, 2019

"...this petty pace"

I wait for the spotted dog beside me
to be gone, skinless bones buried
under yard trees in perfect grass
we mow and mourn.

I wait for the father down the road
to finish his fit, at 87,
draped in a flag, tagged out
as if in a game of catch.

I wait for endings of all beginnings
to wrap our lives in
garments whole and safe as armor,
shielding from the naked chill of loss.

Teaching *The Adventures of Huckleberry Finn*

Huck steered by the shape
in his head, expecting Hell,
rowing straight to Heav'n.

The Road Trip

I am planted in the nearly-leather backseat
of our Chevrolet Impala, still perfumed "brand new."
"As soon as your daddy gets here, we'll be ready,"
Mama says, her lips in hot pink bloom.

Mirror down for her to check and dab,
she turns and glances at me,
making sure that everything is perfect
like the map of expectations she has sketched.

"Hurry up," she shouts to Daddy who's locking the storm door,
making his way to the driver's seat, uneasy
as a child on a doctor's visit, awaiting discomfort,
four hours under the wheel of silence and small-talk.

We roam country roads, avoiding interstates.
Mama eyes the pretty houses sitting posed on Main Streets
like girls who bat their lashes and wait to dance.
We stop at country stores for Mama's favorite bottled Cokes.

Daddy clears his throat, sucks his teeth and whistles,
bronzed farmer-arm out the window. He checks
every hill of tobacco, every field of grain,
wishing he were back in his own dirt.

If anyone is watching us, they see three people
miles and miles from home: a man and a woman
who need the child in the back to keep them on course,
the child who asks over and over, "Where are we going?"

Saturdays in Raleigh

Two little girls wait for Saturdays,
for their mothers to pull on wheat-colored
gloves and feathered hats,
hook garters to suntan nylons,
grab at girdles and varicose veins
before the trip to town, thirty miles
to the capital, where the streets
are framed with parking meters
and at least one window
has a tall, lean woman with a fur-trimmed
coat, a careful coif, as still as sunset
posed in wax.

For Grandmother, One Week Before

Grandma lies dying, sucking breath
like sun in snow, leaving paths behind.
Her eyes doze in sockets closed from light: an eclipse.
We watch her twitch in bed and hear her groans;
they rattle and wheeze while we stand above her
like prison guards. Her chains smolder and spit fire.

The Geraniums

Today as I was leaving, I snapped
five red-headed geraniums from
Daddy's porch planters.
Just enough blood to
stain my hateful fingers.
Through the picture window,
he saw me defiling something
he watched grow.
But who should know better
than a farmer and a father,
that what falls in fertile soil
will hold on tight as roots,
to peep through earth again.

Originally published by *The McKinley Review*, Issue 6, Summer 2019

Paring Apples

He pulled the Case knife from his pants pocket,
opened its shell and picked the blade,
the fat, thick one hardest to pull out.
The apple, sitting on the table next to his big chair,

waited to be undressed in the fanciest way.
Daddy took the heavy,
clunking knife to the bright red apple, a tiny
nick then a motion round and round—

perfect, precision-like movements of
hand and knife and fruit.   The peels curled
like little girl ringlets dangling
from the apple's head,

a thin fragile ruffle all in one piece.
He was able to peel the whole
of it in one tedious motion,
never breaking the red ribbon

until it tumbled
whole to his lap
or the trash can held
between his knees.

Originally published by *The Main Street Rag*, Vol. 24, Number 3, Summer 2019

Chocolate Fudge

The heavy-bottomed pot, gun-grey,
full of chocolate, butter
curling the top,
melted and cooling on the back door step.

Mama's in her apron, the kind
no one wears anymore. She dresses
the countertop in wax paper.
I hear the crunching sound

of aluminum foil, the landing
swish on the Formica next
to the brown stovetop.
She knows just the right amount

of Hershey's and sugar and butter,
just the right timing. She removes
the pot from the doorsteps and frets
over its consistency—or brags, depending.

The worn wooden spoon fits
 Mama's grasp. She holds it firmly
 and drops perfect puddles.
 One single pecan caps the top,

like a crowned checker piece.
The pot sits in the sink now, filled with
hot wash water.
We dare not disturb the fudge until it's ready.

Originally published in Cellar 101: *The Best of the Fuquay-Varina Reading Series*, 2011

The Scooting Stool

Mama would go to the garden
early, just after the dew
of dawn, to pick peas or pull
long ears of corn, to snap okra

with a wooden paring knife
and reach deep into the dirt
for new potatoes. She carried
a medium-sized galvanized bucket

for her haul. The handles dropped around
clanging an early morning rhythm.
She brought a small round stool
which had no other use but to scoot

her through the plowed rows
of garden greenery. She squatted,
picked, then slid, shimmying her bottom
over to the next plant,

dragging the stool with her.
She refined the movement: squatted, picked,
then slid to the end, and back down
the other. Stool and bucket.

The Patient

A vegetative state, as if she's waiting for growth.
As if she is going to be picked or pruned or spread
out on a kitchen counter.
Persistent. Something done over and over with
fervor and determination, a continuing state
of nothingness
like the squash curled up in a bowl but never sliced,
never in its place with onions in a hot, cast-iron pan.
Like vine-ripened tomatoes waiting for bacon
and lettuce and mayonnaise but overlooked,
left to rot and sour.
Like peas unshelled or left in the field,
or corn not shucked, hanging on those skeleton-like stalks,
feeding worms and flying bugs.
Or okra, uncut, growing hard as a bullet.
Nothing but a vegetable
that a child refuses to eat from a Sunday plate.

Originally published *The Main Street Rag*, Vol. 24, Number 3, Summer 2019

Barn Leftovers

The big girls looped and handed,
smoked cigarettes or dipped snuff,
talked about Saturday nights,
boys who took them there.
They worked fast and talked hard.
I wanted their jobs.
I wanted to reach and wrap
my hands around tobacco leaves,
making fancy bundles out of them.
I wanted the luxury of completing
one stick and calling for another one,
another chance to tie a perfect row.

"Pick up the scattering," he'd say.
I wanted to spit.
Pick up the scattering, the leftovers.
All brown and shriveled, ground
in dirt under busy feet.
I wonder if Daddy was just trying
to keep me busy and out of the way,
'til quitting time.
Or, was the gathering of parts
where we make whole cloth
of simple thread.

Hunger

She waited her whole youth
for him. Like a seasoned thief,
she'd wait in darkness, wait
until he was alone
and then step into view
with her bag of tools
hoping he needed repair.

Cowboy's Lullaby

He sat back in the grandstand seat
legs spread wide, his body corralled
by weight and age.
Head hung down and weak lids quivering,
he listened to the whistle blow when someone
else made an 8-second ride.

He knew that the little boy on his daddy's knees
was scared a bit by the clown,
that somewhere a mother was praying for a son
to have a good run and tip his hat.
He heard hooves pound the dirt,
and bull ropes played by leathered hands.

These cowboy lullabies rocked him to sleep,
wide-brimmed hat shaded eyes that finally
gave in to a day's rest.
His feet still spread in the center aisle,
a worn boot turned on its side.
So peaceful there, his face a pasture of memories.

The Roses

People dug bomb shelters
deep in peaceful dirt,
and every airplane that flew the sky
was to me, at six years old.
Mr. Khrushchev ready to blow my body up
higher than my backyard swing,
At ten, I planned to hide in the Rose's basement,
beg them to take me in,
not child's play this time.

Then the teenage years burst me open
and heartbreak ripped like a jagged knife,
into the foolish head of puppy love,
a flea bite, water-wet body shaking
with discomfort.
At fifteen, I planned to sneak into the Rose's garage,
crank the engine,
ride their bright blue Olds,
onto the single street of death.

At 56, there was no safety.
The Rose children needed the
basement to store their early lives,
thinking someone might want their leftovers,
might play pool again
or kiss in the big green chair
hidden in the darkest corner,
and Mr. Jimmy, with his companion cancer,
needed the garage for a dying bedroom,
the Olds traded in for the saddest space.

At 65, plans soured and quick exits disappeared,
I stuffed memories into luggage,
folded them as tight as starched shirts,
forcing a fit,
boxed my life like an unopened gift,
and waited for the moving God to pick me up,

take me past the Roses' home,
(a "for sale" sign in the empty yard,)
the basement and garage gone dark.
and no one planning anything.

At the Train Tracks

Doesn't everyone who waits for a speeding train's approach
Think,
> while sitting there, stopped and lulled
> by the gravely roar of train on tracks,
> beating the steady rhythm of impatient thumbs
> rapping on the steering wheel,
Of saying ready-set-go and stomping the gas,
> riding the underbelly of the iron horse,
> galloping quickly through the darkness,
> letting reins go for dear life,
> landing where there is no waiting.

Squirrel at the Drive-Thru

For three days I watched a squirrel
climb and jump swiftly from tree to tree,
searching for the spot that bears
his meal.

I sat at a drive-thru
waiting for my sandwich. I did not have
to crawl, wiggle, or hustle,
just reached out to grab a fat bag of food.

I chewed and watched him planning his
next jump. I wondered if he
had other trees to search,
wondered if this was the same squirrel.

I remember the old folks saying
"He is barking up the wrong tree,"
and I think about hound dogs,
 their noses twitching for the smell of a 'coon.

They will sit there for hours
Barking, begging for a fight.
They will not give up until
their master pulls them away.

I wondered why, in the beginning of a hunt,
the little squirrels didn't find a nearby limb
to squirm down and tell the hounds
they were "barking up the wrong tree."

Squirrels should be kind enough to
show the dogs and coons some mercy,
The squirrel I was watching didn't seem
smart enough to understand that.

Lazy squirrel is dumb as I am,
holding food and drink between my legs.
not balancing as well as the squirrel,
waiting for someone to do the hunting for me.

Teaching *The Great Gatsby*

Green stone, like cheap beads,
skips the water, tarnishing,
color of cat eyes.

Faith Unlocks the Door

Avon died at the Citgo station,
choked his heart on a biscuit there,
deaf wife beside him.
wanting to hear him speak.

He had prayed for a dog
on the trip to this new home,
knowing a farm would be safe
for mutts and strays.

For exactly one day we had seen the Beagle
in the pasture across the road.
She guarded the rental house,
as if expecting someone.

"Girl" was waiting,
white with a black patch chasing
from tail to spine. She sat there,
having a sense that someone would come.

Happy Birthday, Dad

We would have a huge party if you were here,
100 balloons for every year,
a cake as big as Texas,
and all the buddies you held dear.

You meant to make it ten more years,
though I told you I didn't know if
I could take it that much longer.
Wishing now that you were here.

You made me tough,
gave me useful things,
stubbornness and carelessness
among them for sure.

Those are questionable qualities,
I guess. But it meant
"Standing your ground,"
living without worry on your back.

What made you the happiest
was people, especially if they
would let you pat them, shake their hand,
and answer when you called them, "Old Buddy."

You made me proud most of the time,
but no more than when you rode into a rodeo arena,
your hat in the air and chaps flapping,
with Old Bunk circling fast and spectacular.

I loved you when I saw nieces, nephews
and little cowboys sitting on your lap,
look up at you with as much adoration
as if you had been John Wayne.

We laughed when you talked about San Francisco
and the Golden Gate Bridge.
You said, "my barracks were right there;
just turn left after crossing the bridge."

At 85, you stood outside your barrack door,
excited and touched to tell the story
of your time there and how much you
missed home. You were a proud soldier.

We doubted your proclaimed relationship
with General Macarthur. You pumped
his gas ONE time and that turned
into a lifelong friendship, though one-sided.

The General said, "I shall return,"
and I keep thinking you just might
do the same.
I know you would if you could.

90 years was just not enough for you.
There are new cowpokes to hold
and new nephews to tease,
more grand entries awaiting.

I look for you to cross the pond dam
riding in the latest beat-up Chevrolet
with all four Dalmatians in the back,
adoring you, as animals did,

But I suspect I won't see you,
though I know you are there somewhere.
Every day you are gone is a day
I am closer to you.

The Chandelier

The weeping willow in my front yard
breathes again.
I stop to look at its slender arms
shading the wind-rippled pond.
The tree is not yet fully frocked in green,
but graceful and intricate like a chandelier
in a fancy living room,
shining light on all the promised gold,
and God comfortable in his easy chair, feet up,
reading the book of Life.

Necessary Examination

Life smells like leftover breakfast
or stagnant winter soil.
It is the aggravation of a snagged fingernail,
constantly dripping water
or ill-fitted shoes.

I pick at my life as if it is a scab, a sore,
something to be cured, removed,
banished like a thief.
I cannot find it on a map, so I order
my feet to move, but my legs buckle.

I crawl on bumpy ground to find my way
and wonder what those watching see
me struggling to find solace
in the safety of sameness,
or giving in to not belonging at all.

A Night's Rest

The man who raped me slept free last night.
For twenty-eight years he paid for his crime.
I thought that was enough.

Just after it happened,
I was sure I would never sleep again,
still afraid of the knife at my throat,

remembering his threat to cut my head off
and my promise to him that I would not tell.
Squeezing my eyes shut not to recognize him.

But I have spent all these years
grateful that I was left alive,
thankful to him for that.

I fought neither the rape nor the parole.
My fighting power lost its kick
that September night.

Last night as I tried to fall asleep,
I could only think of him and how happy
he must be to lie in a real bed,

free from clanging noises of steel doors,
the constant whistles and demands of
confinement in a state prison.

This morning I cannot understand
why I thought of him and his pleasure
as I lay once more with fear at my throat.

Poem for Faulkner's "Emily"

She is the monument
covered in rust, hair as gray
as Confederate swords and voice as sharp.
Over in the corner of some museum,
dank as basement ground, she warms her baby,
her suckling, her first-born.
Bundled in hunger, its wails hover ghosts.
She feeds it in cups, empty
and barren as steel—a surrogate tea
that poisons crib and cradle
and rocks the past to dust.

Birth, Finally

My father's death gave birth to me.
I who had winked at him with my first glance
opened my eyes wide to watch him die.
His life was too much for me.

I needed to shed the coat of him,
the garment I felt I had to wear,
as if I were naked
and insignificant without his cover.

The fit of him felt uncomfortable
on Father's Day when every preacher
preached about the perfect, faithful,
head-of-the-household,

a mold my father did not fit.
As much as I adored him.
He was just a man, no more
or less than any other,

a fact I realized as he became sick,
weak, and helpless.
Age struck him down
so quickly and unkindly.

The pieces were too scattered
for me to put back together,
both of us incomplete
and only I left to repair myself.

When his eyes became a glare,
mine were forced to open,
to push aside his shadow,
and wander my way alone.

Today's Task

First thing this morning I will look
under the bed. There among big boxes
of baby clothes my mother saved and dust
bunnies held together by age, I might find it.

I can look in the closet filled with my father's
winter coats, vacuum cleaner parts and
the Chamber of Commerce calendar
where unbeknownst to me my mother
recorded my menstrual cycles.

And if not in the closet, then in the kitchen
way up in the highest cabinet where
Mama kept the home-made pickles
and pear preserves. She held
her breath every time I tried to climb
from the wobbly kitchen stool to the counter
to the goodies.

On to the formal dining room, quiet
and regal as a stuffy queen. Surely
I will find what I seek among the silver service
that I have not polished since my mother died,
or in the top drawer of the china cabinet
where I kept tiny envelopes filled with two dollar bills
my grandmother gave me every Christmas.

Growing weary, I think of looking
in the garage utility room
which held daddy's safe, lawn mower parts
and garden tools, certain that in a cob-webbed corner
I would find what I was searching for.
When I saw the shovel, I realized that seeking
happiness was like little kids digging for China.

Student at the Piano

James plays "Precious Lord,"
striking sharps and flats,
moving to melody,
syncopating the soul,
singing salvation,
while 100 black hands hum him
in white plank churches,
praising the Lord
to the beat of black and white on time.

The Fishermen's Story

People who fish are like children
believing in the Tooth Fairy,
who rarely take "no" for an answer.

They have been told there are fish
in the little pond behind the house.
But, it's a secret. They believe

the fish will only bite for them
because they are the good people;
they deserve to catch a big one.

They stand there watching water,
waiting for a little red ball to pop
up and down, up and down,

and there will be a quick pulling,
and chasing swell in ripples.
Their hands grip the rod, fighting

the fish, big or small, onto land,
saying, "he's a keeper," or "throw him back,"
a quick decision that they make.

And if they miss the bite today,
they will be back. Fishermen are like that;
they throw and wait and whistle.

They blame the wind, the heat,
the hunger of the fish,
but they will be back,

no matter what.
They will be back to sit and wait
for a fish or a good story.

Teaching "Wakefield"

Wakefield walked away
from his spot and watched the world
swallow the empty.

The Funeral Dreams

You steal away from the casket,
a child slipping out of bed at night.
You walk around, full bodied,
glaring at the mourners one by one.
I am busy begging you to stay put.
They do not see or hear you,

but you speak to the grief-stricken.
You are brave enough now to use
weapon words to
claw them like a wild animal,
leaving blood to match their tears:
reminders of misdeeds and exclusions.

Your arms slip out of sockets,
slide to the edge, then thump
to the ground.
Legs drop from their hip bones,
and drag your feet on a wayward rug.
The neck wobbles and your head pops off.

Preachers, in their honey-thick voices,
relieve the pain with proclamations of peace,
and blessed assurance that there is an angel
waiting to greet the dead,
to watch as they gain a gown of clouds
for their journey to the promised place.

But I have seen you crawl from that comfort.
You don't rest easy, and you have gone nowhere.
The bed is stifling; you suffer in that silent cocoon.
There is no going back and no going forward.
You are stuck but won't give up the escape.
You would not take Death lying down.

Missing Pieces

I spent Sunday in my easy chair,
listening to Billy Collins talk
about writing poetry.

Collins admits that as a very young man
he thought it would be cool to be a poet.
Though riddled by age, I think so too.

Poets, he said, are on the inside looking out,
seeing all the special things in things
that others do not see.

I sit on the inside waiting for my inside
to find the perfect words to pull it out,
lay it out to be studied and admired.

But it may be outside where my inside thrives,
in the sunlit pleasure of lazy turtles
covering pond rocks and lily pads.

Or, as the deer clear fences
in proud dancers' leaps
towards the thicket's sanctuary.

It could be me who longs to share smells
like white, sun-dried linens, fresh rain,
and puppy breath kisses.

Identifying with graceful deer and falling rain,
may, to some, seem banal and unworthy
coming from a would-be poet.

I think Billy would say that whatever
you find inside, whatever metaphors you collect,
you must carry with you from flesh to word.

It's like finding what's been missing
when you have turned the house inside out
and looked everywhere but where it is.

A Child's Assignment

As an only child, my homework was clear:
to make them love each other as much as they loved me.

I was to push two heavy walls together, walls
that fought hard every day to stand alone.

I was to tame the ferocious dog in the yard next door
and make him love the fat, furry feline

who needed no playmates.
It was my assignment to bring together oil and water,

and with the magic of a child, make them not only
mix but swirl in a happy dance.

It was my assignment to find the last puzzle piece
that would make the puzzle whole, make every jagged piece

fit together as smoothly as a well-painted wall in a room
where a fire shared the warmth,

and couches held the family cozy,
giving me some time to rest in my own place.

Cows Wading

Nothing looks more amusing
than a few cows
standing in a farm pond
on the hottest summer days
still as statues
unmoved by any other need
but to cool off.
Cows give in
to the discomfort, their sense
of cow pride.
They lumber into the water slowly,
as if they had all day.
They don't splash, hardly disturbing the water at all.
No moos, no tail swishings,
no movement. Perfect eyes are content
shaded by the longest lashes.

Grandpa's Mules

I do not know mules like Grandpa did,
the gee-whinney,
the swish tune of fanning tail,
the shake of ears at flies
and green leaf flowers tickling.

Grandpa closed his eyes
back to that land
down beyond the fishing pond,
the sand slipping under tow-bagged sleds
he made with cola caps,
the mule, head down,
plodding back rows level.

Back to that fertile soil,
Sweat and sweeping gardens
on backyard plots,
an old straw hat set to tilt the sun,
and mule muscles pulling and stretching
a day's work,
when hours played in shadow, passing in the quiet.
"Were they really stubborn?"
"'Bout like children. You had to know how to handle them."

Works Cited

"All in an Ordinary Day." *Floyd County Moonshine*, Vol. 11, Issue 1, Spring 2019.

"Apples." *The Main Street Rag*, Vol. 24, Number 3, Summer 2019.

"Aunt Pauline at 83." *Noctua Review*, Vol. XII, 2019.

"The Blue Top – 1960." *Toasted Cheese Literary Journal*, March, 2019.

"Chocolate Fudge." *Cellar 101: The Best of the Fuquay-Varina Reading Series* 2011, 2011.

"Crossing the Pond Dam." *Rat's Ass Review*, Summer, 2019.

"Geraniums." *The McKinley Review*, Issue 6, Summer 2019.

"Last Request." *Toasted Cheese Literary Journal*, March, 2019.

"The Patient." *The Main Street Rag*, Vol. 24, Number 3, Summer 2019.

"Seasons." *Poet Lore*, Vol. 106, Number 3/4.

"Uncles." *The McKinley Review*, Issue 6, Summer 2019

"Waiting." *From the Edge Poetry Magazine*, Spring 2019.

Teresa McLamb Blackmon grew up in Benson, a small town southeast of Raleigh. She received her MA in English from North Carolina State University and her MLS from North Carolina Central University. She taught high school English for 29 years, and in that time, was publication adviser for newspaper, yearbook, and literary magazine. Now retired, she spends her time writing poetry, knitting, and facilitating a new book club in her hometown. The publication of this, her first book of poems, is a dream come true.

www.ingramcontent.com/pod-product-compliance
Lightning Source LLC
Chambersburg PA
CBHW021158090426
42740CB00008B/1142